Priceless Proverbs
Book 2

Kristi Porter

Copyright © 2014 Happi Kamper Press

ISBN: 0692304185
ISBN-13: 978-0692304181

CONTENTS

Dedication

This book is dedicated to every parent, grandparent, and caregiver that entrusted me with the care and education of their child over the years.

We've all earned a good laugh.

And to the Happi Kamper Kids, the preschoolers at Community United Methodist Preschool, and the Power Play Kids, who all had a part in providing me with material for this book.

Keep smiling and providing those laughs!

The Story Behind This Book

Priceless Proverbs - Book 2, continues where book one left off - with over one hundred additional kid quotes and illustrations. It is the result of hundreds of interviews with young children ages three to twelve, who were presented with the first half of a famous saying or proverb and then asked to finish it themselves.

It began as part of a larger class project by teacher Kristi Porter and the children of Happi Kamper Child Care, located in North Muskegon, Michigan. Each child was to create an individual gift book for his or her parents, and Priceless Proverbs was simply to be one chapter in each child's book.

Now, the individual answers of the Happi Kamper Kids, as well as those of the children at Community United Methodist Preschool, and the kids of Power Play

Childcare have been combined. Their diverse, candid, and often priceless answers may surprise you, or even make you laugh out loud, as you get a quick glimpse into the amazing and intricate minds of some of the most delightful and fascinating children around. Enjoy!

OLD ENGLISH AND OTHER FAMOUS PROVERBS

It's better to be safe than...
... to look like a pumpkin. Alec, age 5.

~~~~~~~~~~~~~~~~~~~~~~~~~~~~~~~~~~~

Children should be seen and not...
... leave their Legos in daddy's room.Chad, age 3.

~~~~~~~~~~~~~~~~~~~~~~~~~~~~~~~~~~~

It's always darkest before…
… Santa comes.   Denny, age 3.

~~~~~~~~~~~~~~~~~~~~~~~~~~~~~~~~~~~

You can lead a horse to water but...
... what if he can't swim?!? Shayna, age 3.

~~~~~~~~~~~~~~~~~~~~~~~~~~~~~~~~~~~~~

No News is...
... when the paper is still in the mailbox.Collyn, age 4.

~~~~~~~~~~~~~~~~~~~~~~~~~~~~~~~~~~~~~

A bird in the hand is worth...
... it, even if it bites you! Makenna, age 5.

~~~~~~~~~~~~~~~~~~~~~~~~~~~~~~~~~~~~~

Two's company, three's…
… tres. (Spanish for three) Kayleigh, age 3.

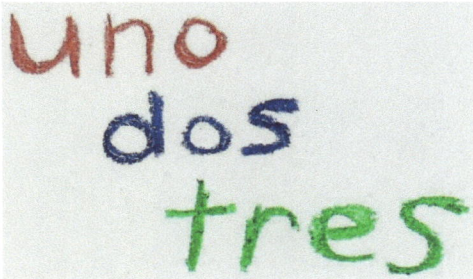

~~~~~~~~~~~~~~~~~~~~~~~~~~~~~~~~~~

What's good for the goose, is…
… probably a good goosing! Logan, age 4.

~~~~~~~~~~~~~~~~~~~~~~~~~~~~~~~~~~

It's never too late to…
… go to McDonalds.   Jennifer, age 4.

~~~~~~~~~~~~~~~~~~~~~~~~~~~~~~~~~~

Give a man enough rope and…
…he can make a swing for me. Tyler, age 4.

~~~~~~~~~~~~~~~~~~~~~~~~~~~~~~~~~~~~~~

The early bird gets…
…the girl bird, if he's lucky.   Troy, age 4.

~~~~~~~~~~~~~~~~~~~~~~~~~~~~~~~~~~~~~~

A miss is as good as a…
… king or queen. Alicia, age 4.

~~~~~~~~~~~~~~~~~~~~~~~~~~~~~~~~~~~~~~

If you can't beat them...
... you lose!   Kyle, age 4.

~~~~~~~~~~~~~~~~~~~~~~~~~~~~~~~~~~~

Let sleeping dogs...
... alone, or they will bite your hand off! Emma, age 4.

~~~~~~~~~~~~~~~~~~~~~~~~~~~~~~~~~~~

Bad news travels...
... on my mom's phone. Austin, age 4.

~~~~~~~~~~~~~~~~~~~~~~~~~~~~~~~~~~~

Practice what you…
…have to do for the dance show! Brielle, age 4.

~~~~~~~~~~~~~~~~~~~~~~~~~~~~~~~~~~~

The best things in life are…
... what God gives you.   Jaley, age 4.

~~~~~~~~~~~~~~~~~~~~~~~~~~~~~~~~~~~

Silence is…
… *never* at my house!   Chase, age 4.

~~~~~~~~~~~~~~~~~~~~~~~~~~~~~~~~~~~

Once bitten…
… smack the kid!   Dennis, age 12.

~~~~~~

You can catch more flies with honey than…
… by chasing them on your bike. Devin, age 8.

~~~~~~

A stitch in time saves…
… about a dime?   Emilia, age 4.

~~~~~~

It's better to be safe than…

… to play with alligators, tigers, & lions. Elizabeth, age 4.

~~~~~~~~~~~~~~~~~~~~~~~~~~~~~~~~~~~

It's always darkest before…

… the smokestack blows. Jake, age 3.

~~~~~~~~~~~~~~~~~~~~~~~~~~~~~~~~~~~

You can lead a horse to water but...

... why? Tony, age 3.

~~~~~~~~~~~~~~~~~~~~~~~~~~~~~~~~~~~

No News is…

…on the weather channel - it's just weather. Madison, age 5.

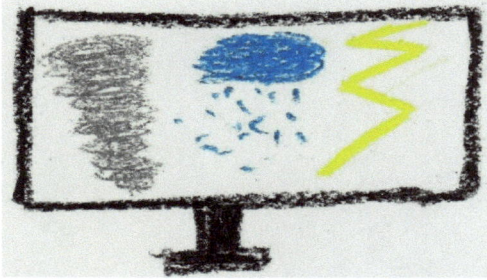

~~~~~~~~~~~~~~~~~~~~~~~~~~~~~~~~~~~~

A bird in the hand is worth…

… my mother. Jacob, age 5.

~~~~~~~~~~~~~~~~~~~~~~~~~~~~~~~~~~~~

Two's company, three's…

... how old I am. Clare, age 3.

~~~~~~~~~~~~~~~~~~~~~~~~~~~~~~~~~~~~

What's good for the goose, is…
… a Mrs. Goose. Zack, age 5.

~~~~~~~~~~~~~~~~~~~~~~~~~~~~~~~~~~~

It's never too late to…
… fight with your brother. Matthew, age 4.

~~~~~~~~~~~~~~~~~~~~~~~~~~~~~~~~~~~

Give a man enough rope and…
…some food and water too. Donovan, age 8.

~~~~~~~~~~~~~~~~~~~~~~~~~~~~~~~~~~~

The early bird gets…

…the best tree & biggest nest. Shane, age 4.

~~~~~~~~~~~~~~~~~~~~~~~~~~~~~~~~~~~~

A miss is as good as a…

… mister. Haley, age 5.

~~~~~~~~~~~~~~~~~~~~~~~~~~~~~~~~~~~~

If you can't beat them…

…just ride a motorcycle. Connor, age 4.

~~~~~~~~~~~~~~~~~~~~~~~~~~~~~~~~~~~~

Let sleeping dogs…

…borrow your blankie to sleep on. Veronica, age 3.

~~~~~~~~~~~~~~~~~~~~~~~~~~~~~~~~~~~~~

Bad news travels…

… in a big truck, sometimes. Leah, age 4.

~~~~~~~~~~~~~~~~~~~~~~~~~~~~~~~~~~~~~

Practice what you…

…say to girls. Gunnar, age 4.

~~~~~~~~~~~~~~~~~~~~~~~~~~~~~~~~~~~~~

The best things in life are…
... ice cream and summer. Kate, age 6.

~~~~~~~~~~~~~~~~~~~~~~~~~~~~~~~~~~~~

Silence is…
… when mom yells "stop the noise!!" Aiden, age 4.

~~~~~~~~~~~~~~~~~~~~~~~~~~~~~~~~~~~~

Once bitten…
… by an alligator, you will *never* forget it! Bella, age 4.

~~~~~~~~~~~~~~~~~~~~~~~~~~~~~~~~~~~~

You can catch more flies with honey than…
… with your hands. Gabrielle, age 4.

~~~~~~~~~~~~~~~~~~~~~~~~~~~~~~~~~~~~

Children should be seen & not…
… left in the woods. Anthony, age 4.

~~~~~~~~~~~~~~~~~~~~~~~~~~~~~~~~~~~~

A stitch in time saves…
… stuff from blowing up.   Evan, age 5.

~~~~~~~~~~~~~~~~~~~~~~~~~~~~~~~~~~~~

ACTUAL PROVERBS (For Reference)

It's better to be safe than sorry. ~Old English Proverb

Children should be seen and not heard. ~Old English Proverb

It's always darkest before the dawn. ~Old English Proverb

You can lead a horse to water but you cannot make him drink. ~Old English Proverb

**No news is good news.* ~French Proverb

A bird in the hand is worth two in the bush. ~Old English Proverb

Two's company, three's a crowd. ~American Proverb

What's good for the goose is good for the gander. ~Originally written as "That that's good sauce for a goose, is good for a gander." in 1670 in John Ray's A Collection of Proverbs.

It's never too late to mend. ~Old English Proverb

Give a man enough rope and he will hang himself. ~Old English Proverb

The early bird gets the worm. ~Old English Proverb

A miss is as good as a mile. ~Old English Proverb

If you can't beat them, join them. ~American idiom based on Scottish proverb

Let sleeping dogs lie. ~Old English Proverb

Bad news travels fast. ~Old English Proverb

The best things in life are free. ~American Proverb

Practice what you preach. ~Old English Proverb

Silence is golden. ~One half of a German Proverb originally written as - 'Speech is silver, but silence is golden.'

Once bitten, twice shy. ~Old English Proverb

You can catch more flies with honey than vinegar. ~Old English Proverb

A stitch in time saves nine. ~Old English Proverb

BEN FRANKLIN QUOTES

If you lie down with the dogs, you will…
… get dog poop on your bed. Emily, age 4.

~~~~~~~~~~~~~~~~~~~~~~~~~~~~~~~~~~~~

A fool and his money are…
… always good for cash. Isabella, age 4.

~~~~~~~~~~~~~~~~~~~~~~~~~~~~~~~~~~~~

People who live in a glass house shouldn't…
… *ever* go to the bathroom! Grace, age 4.

~~~~~~~~~~~~~~~~~~~~~~~~~~~~~~~~~~~~

A small leak will…
…keep dripping until you fix it. Maddie, age 4.

~~~~~~~~~~~~~~~~~~~~~~~~~~~~~~~~~~~~

Early to bed, early to rise, makes a man…
… get to work *way* to early. Ben, age 7.

~~~~~~~~~~~~~~~~~~~~~~~~~~~~~~~~~~~~

A penny saved is…
… not enough.   Tess, age 4.

~~~~~~~~~~~~~~~~~~~~~~~~~~~~~~~~~~~~

No pain, no...

... sunburn lotion.   Clark, age 5.

~~~~~~~~~~~~~~~~~~~~~~~~~~~~~~~~~~~~

A fool and his money are...

...going to Walmart.   Ansley, age 4.

~~~~~~~~~~~~~~~~~~~~~~~~~~~~~~~~~~~~

If you lie down with the dogs, you will...

... probably get smushed. Hailey, age 4.

~~~~~~~~~~~~~~~~~~~~~~~~~~~~~~~~~~~~

Three may keep a secret if…
…they don't tell my mom.   Caleb, age 4.

~~~~~~~~~~~~~~~~~~~~~~~~~~~~~~~~~~~~~

People who live in a glass house shouldn't…
… let the dog inside.   Noah, age 4.

~~~~~~~~~~~~~~~~~~~~~~~~~~~~~~~~~~~~~

A small leak will…
… still make a big mess. Sophia, age 4.

~~~~~~~~~~~~~~~~~~~~~~~~~~~~~~~~~~~~~

Early to bed, early to rise, makes a man…
… really, really cranky. Joey, age 7.

~~~~~~~~~~~~~~~~~~~~~~~~~~~~~~~~~~~

A penny saved is…
…why my daddy goes to work. Katie, age 4.

~~~~~~~~~~~~~~~~~~~~~~~~~~~~~~~~~~~

No pain, no…
… going to the doctor. Lisa, age 5.

~~~~~~~~~~~~~~~~~~~~~~~~~~~~~~~~~~~

Whatever is begun in anger, ends...

…with a time out. Leighton, age 4.

~~~~~~~~~~~~~~~~~~~~~~~~~~~~~~~~~~~~

Never leave until tomorrow what...

… your mom says you have to do today. Ella, age 4.

~~~~~~~~~~~~~~~~~~~~~~~~~~~~~~~~~~~~

Three may keep a secret if...

…they all stay in the car. Allie, age 4.

~~~~~~~~~~~~~~~~~~~~~~~~~~~~~~~~~~~~

ACTUAL BEN FRANKLIN QUOTES
(For Reference)

If you lie down with the dogs, you will rise up with fleas. ~Benjamin Franklin

A fool and his money are soon parted. ~Benjamin Franklin

People who live in glass houses shouldn't throw stones. ~Benjamin Franklin

A small leak can sink a great ship. ~Benjamin Franklin

Early to bed, early to rise, makes a man healthy, wealthy, and wise. ~Benjamin Franklin

A penny saved is a penny earned. ~Benjamin Franklin

No pain, no gain. ~American Adage based on a quote by Benjamin Franklin "There is no gain without pain."

Never leave that till tomorrow that which you can do today.   ~ Benjamin Franklin

Whatever is begun in anger, ends in shame. ~Benjamin Franklin

Three may keep a secret if two of them are dead. ~Benjamin Franklin

OTHER FAMOUS SAYINGS AND QUOTES

Where there's smoke, there's…
… probably cigarettes. Becky, age 4.

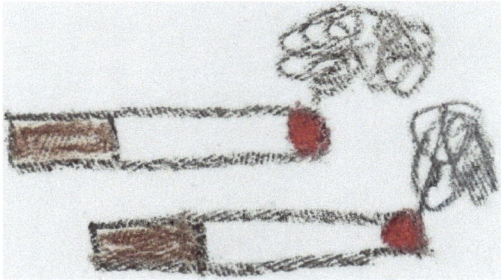

~~~~~~~~~~~~~~~~~~~~~~~~~~~~~~~~~~

If at first you don't succeed…
… it's 'cause you didn't read the rules. Annie, age 5.

~~~~~~~~~~~~~~~~~~~~~~~~~~~~~~~~~~

Don't bite the hand that…
… is this one. (shows hand) Isabelle, age 3.

~~~~~~~~~~~~~~~~~~~~~~~~~~~~~~~~~~

The pen is mightier than the…
… pencil sharpener. Hunter, age 4.

~~~~~~~~~~~~~~~~~~~~~~~~~~~~~~~~~~~~

Speak softly and carry a big…
… hammer. Luci, age 4.

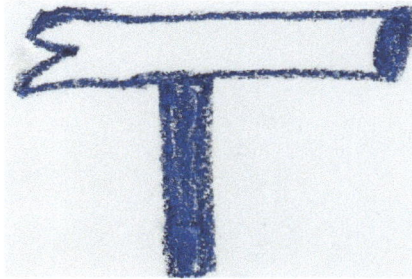

~~~~~~~~~~~~~~~~~~~~~~~~~~~~~~~~~~~~

Look before you…
… crack the egg in the wrong bowl. Wesley, age 5.

~~~~~~~~~~~~~~~~~~~~~~~~~~~~~~~~~~~~

The only thing we have to fear is…

…terrorists. William, age 5.

~~~~~~~~~~~~~~~~~~~~~~~~~~~~~~~~~~~~

Where there's a will, there's…

… a grandpa. Layla, age 5.

~~~~~~~~~~~~~~~~~~~~~~~~~~~~~~~~~~~~

You can't judge a book by…

…what your sister says. Nickolas, age 4.

~~~~~~~~~~~~~~~~~~~~~~~~~~~~~~~~~~~~

You can't teach an old dog...
...that almost died, *anything*! Tommy, age 5.

~~~~~~~~~~~~~~~~~~~~~~~~~~~~~~~~~~~~

If you can't stand the heat...
...go stand in front of the freezer, like my mom. Rylee, age 4.

~~~~~~~~~~~~~~~~~~~~~~~~~~~~~~~~~~~~

The only way to have a friendis to...
...give them candy. Justine, age 4.

~~~~~~~~~~~~~~~~~~~~~~~~~~~~~~~~~~~~

Don't cry over…

…rainy weather, 'cause rain makes the grass grow.
Charles, age 7.

~~~~~~~~~~~~~~~~~~~~~~~~~~~~~~~~~~~~~~

It ain't over until…

… you die. Joseph, age 8.

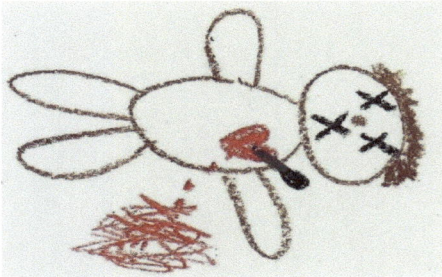

~~~~~~~~~~~~~~~~~~~~~~~~~~~~~~~~~~~~~~

The bigger they are, the harder…

… they are to bite. Iliza, age 4.

~~~~~~~~~~~~~~~~~~~~~~~~~~~~~~~~~~~~~~

It takes two, to…
…play the good video games. Jeremy, age 8.

~~~~~~

When it rains, it…
…gets everything sopping wet! Abbey, age 3.

~~~~~~

A friend is someone who has…
… *lots* of chickens. Jaegar, age 4.

~~~~~~

Strike while the…
…ump says there are no outs. Parker age 4.

~~~~~~~~~~~~~~~~~~~~~~~~~~~~~~~~~~

Never underestimate the power of…
… getting hit in the head. Christian, age 4.

~~~~~~~~~~~~~~~~~~~~~~~~~~~~~~~~~~

Eat, drink, and …
…then go wink at someone! Chelsea, age 9.

~~~~~~~~~~~~~~~~~~~~~~~~~~~~~~~~~~

Don't bite the hand that...
...moves, or it will smack you! Jimmy, age 4.

~~~~~~

Where there's smoke, there's...
...smoke alarms beeping I hope! Makayla, age 4.

~~~~~~

Look before you...
... talk bad about people. Justin, age 9.

~~~~~~

Speak softly and carry a big…

… bottle of water. Meagan, age 4.

~~~~~~

The pen is mightier than the…

… blue one, the red one is the mighty one. Michelle, age 5.

~~~~~~

It ain't over until…

… mom turns it off. Kylie, age 4.

~~~~~~

The only thing we have to fear is...

… girls, definitely girls.   Wyatt, age 5.

~~~~~~~~~~~~~~~~~~~~~~~~~~~~~~~~~~~~~

Where there's a will, there's...

… usually lots of words. Lily, age 8.

~~~~~~~~~~~~~~~~~~~~~~~~~~~~~~~~~~~~~

You can't judge a book by...

…just looking at its pictures. Ashley, age 4.

~~~~~~~~~~~~~~~~~~~~~~~~~~~~~~~~~~~~~

You can't teach an old dog...
...how to brush his own teeth. Josie, age 4.

~~~~~~

If you can't stand the heat...
...try standing on your head. Makenzie, age 4.

~~~~~~

The only way to have a friend is to...
...not hit them. Topanga, age 4.

~~~~~~

Don't cry over…
…stupid stuff. Save it for when somebody dies.
Daniel, age 10.

~~~~~~~~~~~~~~~~~~~~~~~~~~~~~~~~~

Never underestimate the power of…
… policemen. Garrett, age 4.

~~~~~~~~~~~~~~~~~~~~~~~~~~~~~~~~~

The bigger they are, the harder…
… it is to go around them. Malaina, age 4.

~~~~~~~~~~~~~~~~~~~~~~~~~~~~~~~~~

It takes two, to…
… wake my dad up. Emmalee, age 4.

~~~~~~~~~~~~~~~~~~~~~~~~~~~~~~~~~~~~~~~

When it rains, it…
… means I can't play outside. Ryan, age 4.

~~~~~~~~~~~~~~~~~~~~~~~~~~~~~~~~~~~~~~~

A friend is someone who has…
… a big heart. Meggan, age 5.

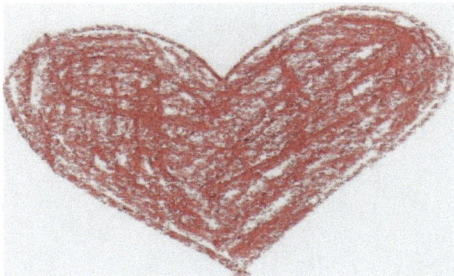

~~~~~~~~~~~~~~~~~~~~~~~~~~~~~~~~~~~~~~~

Strike while the...
... mom is not looking. Samantha, age 5.

~~~~~~

Eat, drink, and ...
... watch TV until bedtime. Gavin, age 4.

~~~~~~

If at first you don't succeed...
... stop, drop and roll! Ethan, age 3.

~~~~~~

OTHER FAMOUS SAYINGS & QUOTES
(For Reference)

Where there's smoke, there's fire. ~American Adage based on the quote of John Lyly, "There can no great smoke arise, but there must be some fire."

If at first you don't succeed, try, then try again. ~Mason Cooley

Don't bite the hand that feeds you. ~Popular idiom that originated with the Aesop's Fables tale - The Dog in the Manger.

The pen is mightier than the sword. ~Edward Bulwer-Lytton

Speak softly and carry a big stick. ~Theodore Roosevelt

Look before you leap. ~Samuel Butler

The only thing we have to fear is fear itself. ~Franklin D. Roosevelt

Where there's a will, there's a way. ~Général Charles de Gaulle

You can't judge a book by its cover. ~American Idiom based on the writings of François Rabelais, "Don't read only the cheerful titles of books. You have to actually open a book and carefully weigh what's written there."

You can't teach an old dog new tricks. ~E. C. Brewer

If you can't stand the heat get out of the kitchen. ~Harry Truman

The only way to have a friend is to be one. ~Ralph Waldo Emerson

Don't cry over spilt milk. ~European fairy folklore. The belief was that fairies enjoyed drinking spilled milk, so the loss of the spilt milk was for good use and not a terrible waste.

It ain't over until the fat lady sings. ~Colloquialism first attributed to sports journalist Ralph Carpenter on March 10,1976, during the SWC tournament finals.

The bigger they are, the harder they fall. ~American boxer Robert Fitzsimmons in an interview in 1902.

It takes two to tango. ~A song title from 1952,that became a popular American idiom.

When it rains, it pours. ~Sourced from an old proverb 'It never rains but it pours,' the modern version, "When it rains, it pours" was the creation of the Morton Salt company, whose crystallized salt didn't clump in humid weather.

A friend is someone who has the same enemies you have. ~Abraham Lincoln

Strike while the iron is hot. ~Francis Rabelais

Eat, drink and be merry. ~From the Bible, Ecclesiastes VIII 15 (King James Version)

Never underestimate the power of a woman. ~Popular advertising slogan by *Ladies Home Journal*, beginning with the March 1941 issue.

###

A NOTE FROM THE AUTHOR

I love hearing from my readers, and I answer all my mail personally. If you enjoyed this book, would you be kind enough to leave a review on Amazon? Even if it's only a few words - it really does make a difference, and would be very much appreciated.

Simply go to www.amazon.com, and type Kristi Porter into the search bar. Then choose the appropriate story, click reviews, create your own review, and let me know what you thought.

~ ~ ~

If you would like to receive an automatic email when my next book is released, go to http://eepurl.com/ES3kD to sign up. Your email address will never be shared and you can unsubscribe at any time.

~ ~ ~

Thanks so much for taking the time to read and review my work. It's readers like you that help make my next book even better!

Kristi Porter

OTHER BOOKS BY KRISTI PORTER
Available at Amazon.com and bookstores everywhere.

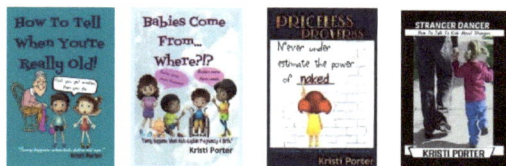

How to Tell When You're Really Old - Funny Happens When Kids Define Old Age, is the result of hundreds of interviews with children ages three to twelve, who were asked to explain how they could tell when someone was really old. Their candid, uncensored, and often hilarious answers will not only make you rethink the aging process, but are sure to become instant favorites for readers of all ages.

~ ~ ~

Babies Come From... Where?!? Funny Happens When Kids Explain Pregnancy & Birth is the result of hundreds of interviews with children ages three to twelve, who were simply asked "Where do you think babies come from?" and allowed to answer freely, giving as much or as little explanation as they saw fit. Now, their candid, uncensored and often hilarious answers have been collected and made available for all to enjoy in this delightful little book that is sure to be a favorite for years to come.

~ ~ ~

Priceless Proverbs - Funny Happens When Kids Finish Famous Sayings is a clever collection of words and crayon art created by children of today. Honest and raw, this small book is an utter delight as each old saying or proverb is revised and filtered through the innocent minds of children ages 3 to 12. Sayings that have become so clichéd to we adults, take on a totally new twist as children tend to tell it as it is, and you're certain to find delightful surprises on every page. Highly relatable, this book will make you want to interview the kid closest to you for even more "Priceless Proverbs!"

~ ~ ~

Stranger Danger - How to Talk to Kids About Strangers is a guide to help parents and caregivers of children ages 3-8 teach kids about strangers in a fun, interactive, and age appropriate way - without scaring them. This easy to read, step by step guide gives parents age appropriate words and activities to use with even the youngest of children. Covering everything from who is a stranger, to when and how to fight back, *Stranger Danger - How to Talk to Kids About Strangers* is a must read guide for today's parents.

ABOUT THE AUTHOR

Kristi Porter has over twenty-five years of experience working with young children, both as a preschool teacher, and as an award winning child care provider. She holds a degree in Early Childhood Education and Development, as well as a national Child Development Associate Credential. In 1999, she was awarded the Governor's Quality Care Award for her outstanding commitment to the care and education of young children.

Always a reader, Kristi never thought much about writing until she entered a writing contest sponsored by the Detroit Free Press. Her story - *The Worst Vacation Ever* - went on to be published in a travel anthology that was distributed worldwide. This was followed by numerous articles published in local magazines and newspapers. As her love of writing grew, she added adult fiction, how-to books for parents, and short humor pieces to her repertoire.

But kids and writing aren't all Kristi relishes. She also enjoys bicycling, video games, photography, Facebook, and spending time with family. She lives in Michigan.

CONNECT WITH KRISTI ONLINE

Twitter: @KristiPorter3

Facebook: Facebook/Kristi Porter - Author

Website: http://happikamper.weebly.com

Email: Kristiporter03@gmail.com

ACKNOWLEDGEMENTS

I'd like to extend a warm thanks to Lynn Dahl Scholl, Tish Huber Winton, and Sheri Berge, for helping me conduct hundreds of interviews with children over the years. I couldn't have done it without all of you.

Many thanks as well to the White Lake Writers Group for their guidance, encouragement, and support as I sorted through all of those interviews to put this book together.

A special thanks goes out to Tirzah Goodwin, for her awesome cover design; & to my three amazing grandsons for their help with illustrations.

Lots of love, respect and appreciation to my husband for his understanding and support as I spent countless hours in front of the computer, preparing this book for publication.

And to my mom, for always believing in me, encouraging me, and pestering me to finish this and other projects - I love you more than words can say.

And finally, a heartfelt thank you to the children of North Muskegon, who allowed me into their hearts and minds, and gave me a remarkable glimpse into this wonderful world we live in - thru their eyes, their minds, and their perceptions. Priceless.

www.ingramcontent.com/pod-product-compliance
Lightning Source LLC
Chambersburg PA
CBHW041758040426
42447CB00001B/10